This section of the book focuses on the cc[...]tivities help learners to represent information in the context of a graph. As they create various graphs on their own, learners strengthen their ability to analyze facts.

Reading Charts

The third section of this book deals with the reading and interpreting of charts. The activities are designed to enhance the learner's abilities in assessing presented information. As the learner becomes more confident in answering these questions, he or she reinforces his or her abilities of analyzing and assessing data.

Charting Data

This section entails the creation of charts. The activities are designed to get learners to clearly present information in the form of charts. As the learners construct their own charts, they reinforce their abilities to analyze data. The learners familiarize themselves with the logical manner in which information is assembled into charts. They also begin to comprehend the importance of visually presenting information in a concise way.

Tables

The fifth section of this book orients learners to the mathematical world of tables. By looking at and completing tables, learners will become aware of recurring themes within the products of math equations. Learners will build stronger foundations in the logic and reasoning found throughout the principal theories of basic mathematics.

Visual Puzzles

The last section of this book revisits charts and graphs. However, in this section the context changes. The activities are more thought provoking, reinforcing what the learner has already studied and adding a new level to that understanding by challenging the learner to visually solve new problems.

Name _____

Planes, Trains, and Automobiles

Graphs are drawings or diagrams used to show information such as amount, length, or distance.

Directions: Study the graph below and answer the questions.

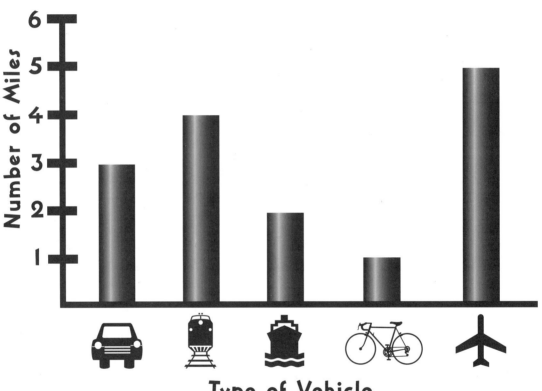

1 Which of these vehicles traveled the longest distance? How many miles did the vehicle travel? _____

2 How much farther did the train travel than the boat? _____

3 What is the shortest distance that any of the vehicles traveled? _____

4 What is the total distance traveled by all five vehicles? _____

Contents

How to Use This Book   2

Pre-assessment Activities
Reading Graphs   4
Graphing Data   5
Reading Charts   6
Charting Data   7
Tables   8
Visual Puzzle   9

Reading Graphs
Teaching Tips   10
Bar Graphs   11
Pictographs   12
Pie Graphs   13
Bar Graphs   14
Post-assessment Activities   15

Graphing Data
Teaching Tips   16
Pictographs   17
Bar Graphs   18
Pie Graphs   19
Pictographs   20
Post-assessment Activities   21

Reading Charts
Teaching Tips   22
Reading Charts   23
Reading Charts   24

Reading Charts   25
Reading Charts   26
Post-assessment Activities   27

Charting Data
Teaching Tips   28
Charting from Data   29
Charting from Pictures   30
Charting from Maps   31
Charting from Maps   32
Post-assessment Activities   33

Tables
Teaching Tips   34
Addition   35
Multiplication   36
Solving Problems   37
Missing Data   38
Post-assessment Activities   39

Visual Puzzles
Teaching Tips   40
Bar Graphs   41
From Chart to Graph   42
Pie Graphs   43
Grids   44
Post-assessment Activities   45

Answer Key   46

How to Use This Book

Mathematical Thinking: Ideas and Procedures is an engrossing, hands-on resource to help learners hone essential math skills. This Brain Builders activity book provides activities designed to reinforce the learner's ability to read and represent data in a clear and logical manner, as well as building the learner's skills of interpreting data presented in math problems. Understanding representation as a means of communication goes hand in hand with educational trends that emphasize developing learners' reasoning abilities. In this book, learners will not only learn to approach math problems based on visual data, but they will also learn to create coherent visual representations of data themselves. By reading and representing data, learners grow analytically while building the critical-thinking foundations necessary for more advanced mathematical problems.

Mathematical Thinking: Ideas and Procedures is comprised of six sections, each emphasizing a different area of the third-grade math curriculum. Each section presents four curriculum-based activities, based on the standards of the National Council of Teachers of Mathematics. The activities highlight key math concepts and skills taught in classrooms across the United States. Activities offer learners easy-to-follow directions as well as skill definitions and examples. The activities also present kid-friendly fun facts to engage learners and show them that math exists in the world around them. Each of the following sections will help your learners to develop their reasoning abilities as they come to understand the visual communication of math concepts and properties that they have learned in the classroom.

Reading Graphs

This section involves the development of the learners' abilities to analyze and comprehend information as presented in the form of graphs. The activities familiarize learners with the structure of various types of graphs. As learners answer questions about the information represented, they build their fluency in the visual language of mathematics.

Graphing Data

In the third grade, learners are not only becoming familiar with the different ways in which information is assembled into graphs, but they begin to understand the logic of representing data in various ways.

2

Name _____

Crawly Things

A bar graph uses bars to show amounts or numbers so that they can be compared.

✏️ **Directions: Fill in the bar graph below to show how many centimeters (cm) the following insects are.**

Ant=1 cm   Beetle=3 cm   Moth=5 cm
Praying mantis=12 cm   Ladybug=1 cm   Centipede=7 cm

1 Which is the longest bar on the graph? _____

2 How many of the bugs on the graph were longer than four centimeters? _____

3 If you placed 4 centipedes together, how long would they be? _____

Name _____

Heavy Weights

Charts can be drawings that show information, such as weight or amount, in an easy-to-see way.

> **Directions: Look at the charts below and answer the following questions.**

Mary

John

Key:
= 10 pounds

Bob

Julie

1 Which student weighs the most? How much does he or she weigh? _____

2 How much does Mary weigh? How much do Mary and Bob weigh together? _____

3 How much more does John weigh than Julie? _____

6

Name _____

Working for the Weekend

✏️ Directions: Place the following information into the chart below.

Sarah and Mindy are baby-sitting to earn money for the weekend. On Monday, Sarah earned $3.10. On Tuesday, she earned $2.50, on Wednesday she earned $1.75, and on Thursday she earned $5.40. On Monday, Mindy earned $2.50. On Tuesday she earned $4.80, on Wednesday she earned $2.70, and on Thursday she earned $3.25.

	Monday	Tuesday	Wednesday	Thursday
Sarah				
Mindy				

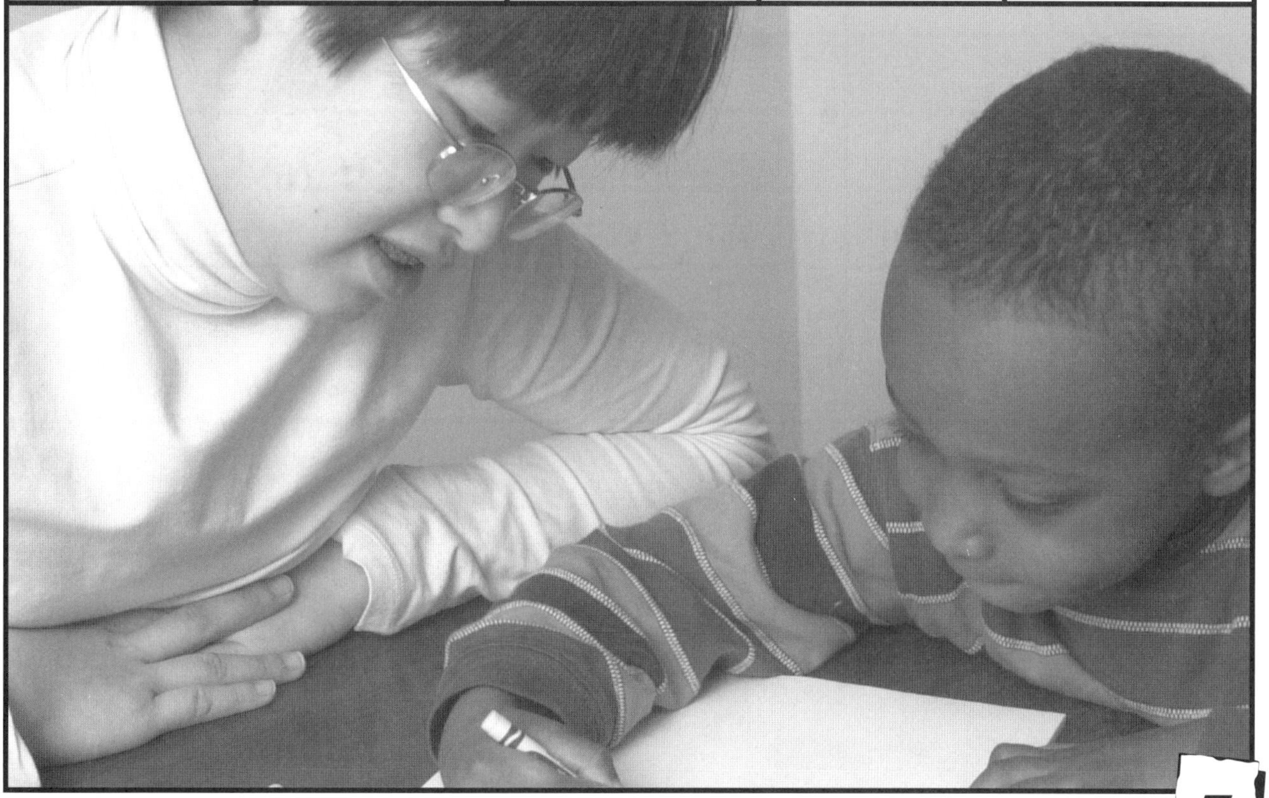

Name _____

Setting the Table

A table organizes mathematical information into columns and rows.

✏️ **Directions: Complete these addition and multiplication tables.**

+	0	1	2	3	4	5
0						
1		2				
2			4			
3				6		
4					8	
5						10

X	1	2	3	4	5
1				4	
2			6		
3		6			
4	4				
5				20	

1 When an even number is added to an
   even number, is the answer odd or even? _____

2 What happens to a number
   when it is added with zero? _____

Name _____

We the People

> **Directions:** People go to Washington, D.C., to visit historical monuments and buildings such as the Washington Monument, the Capitol, the White House, the Tomb of the Unknown Soldier, and the Vietnam Veterans Memorial. Make a bar graph to show how many people visited each place last Saturday.

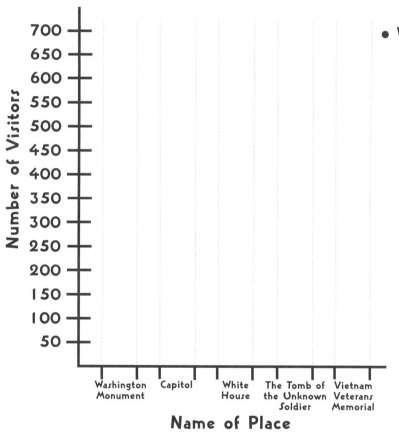

- **Washington Monument** 350 people
- **Capitol** 500 people
- **White House** 250 people
- **The Tomb of the Unknown Soldier** 200 people
- **Vietnam Veterans Memorial** 650 people

1 What was the most visited site? How many more people visited this site than the White House?

_____

2 What was the least visited site? _____

9

Teaching Tips...

TEACHING TIPS

Background

- The ways in which mathematical ideas are represented are important to a learner's understanding of those ideas. Representations should be considered important elements in supporting a student's comprehension of mathematical concepts and relationships. Graphs are visual representations of information such as amount, length, or distance. Giving learners the skills to read graphs and interpret the data represented by those graphs will help them to identify and compare information about varying items.

Homework Helper

- Create a bar graph based upon the weights of objects collected from around the home or classroom. Do not label the bar graph. Present the learners with the objects you have collected and ask them to try and match those objects based upon their weight to the bars on the graph that you have drawn. Explain to the learners that a greater weight is represented by a longer bar on the graph. This allows learners to understand how information is represented in a bar graph.

Research-based Activity

- To build on the activities on pages 12 and 13, ask a learner to look up four different types of animals on the Internet and record the average weight of each. Help the learner to search for the information if necessary. Round the animals' average weights to the nearest ten pounds and have the learner graph the weights of the animals on a bar graph that you have helped them to create.

Test Prep

- The following activities are based on a sampling of national and state standards. It is important for a learner to fully understand how mathematical information can be visually represented in charts and graphs. Once a learner understands how information is represented, that learner can take the next step and chart or graph raw information into a visual format.

Different Audiences

- If you are working with an accelerated learner, create a few additional problems for the learner by increasing the amounts of information in the questions following the activities.

10

Name _____

Mountains of the World

A bar graph uses bars to show amounts or numbers so that they can be compared.

Directions: Study the bar graph below and answer the following questions.

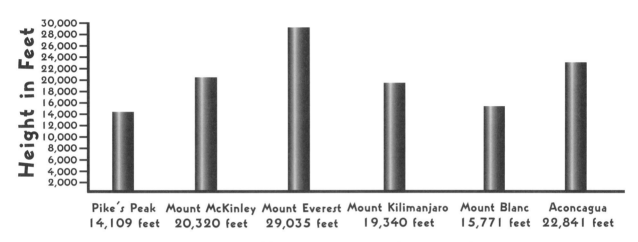

Names of Mountains and their Heights

1 How many mountains are shown on the bar graph? _____

2 Which is the smallest mountain
shown on the bar graph? _____

3 Which is the second tallest mountain? _____

FUN FACT

Mount Everest is the tallest mountain in the world. It rises a few millimeters every year due to movements of the earth.

11

Name _____

Pets

A pictograph, or picture graph, shows information with pictures.

✏️➪ **Directions: Many students at Washington Grammar School have pets. Study the key and the graph below to answer the questions.**

▲ = 5 Pets

Pets	1st graders	2nd graders	3rd graders	4th graders	5th graders
 🐕	▲	▲	▲▲	▲▲▲	▲▲▲▲
 🐈		▲▲	▲▲▲	▲▲▲▲	▲▲▲
 🐟	▲▲▲▲	▲▲▲	▲▲	▲▲▲	▲▲
 🦜	▲▲	▲▲	▲▲▲		▲▲
 🐹	▲▲▲	▲	▲▲	▲	▲▲

1 What does this symbol ▲ stand for? _____

2 How many goldfish do the third graders have? _____

3 Which grade has the largest number of parakeets?
How many do they have? _____

4 What is the total number of pets
belonging to the third graders? _____

5 Which grade has the fewest pets?
Which grade has the most pets? _____

Name _____

The Snake House

A pie graph is a drawing of a circle divided into sections like pieces of a pie.

> **Directions:** Mr. Johnson's class visited the snake house at the zoo and saw many different kinds of snakes. The class saw a total of 20 snakes. Study the pie graph below and answer the following questions.

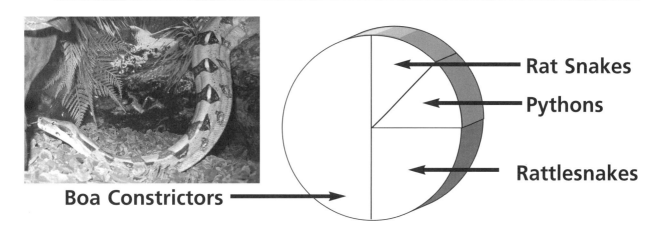

Boa Constrictors

Rat Snakes

Pythons

Rattlesnakes

1 What type of snake did the students see
the most at the snake house? _____

2 What fraction of the total snakes
do boa constrictors represent? _____

3 What fraction of the total snakes
do the rat snakes represent? _____

4 What fraction of the total snakes do the
rat snakes and the pythons represent together? _____

FUN FACT The Inland Taipan of Australia is considered by many experts to be the world's most poisonous snake. A single bite from this snake has enough poison to kill over 100 people.

Name _____

Planets and Moons

A bar graph uses bars to show amounts or numbers so that they can be compared.

Directions: Look at the graph and answer the following questions.

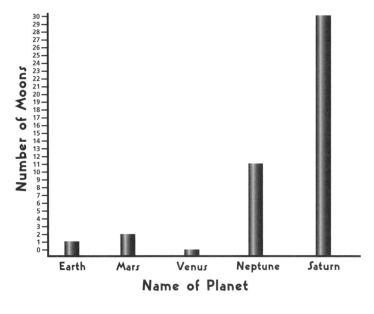

1 What is the subject of this graph? _____

2 Which planet has the most moons?
How many moons does the planet have? _____

3 Which is the planet with
the least number of moons? _____

FUN FACT

The strongest winds on any planet have been measured on Neptune. The winds of Neptune have been found to blow up to 1,250 miles (2,000 km) per hour!

Name _____

Skill Check—Reading Graphs

Bar Graphs

✏️➤ **Directions:** Study the bar graph below and answer the following questions.

The World's Largest Deserts

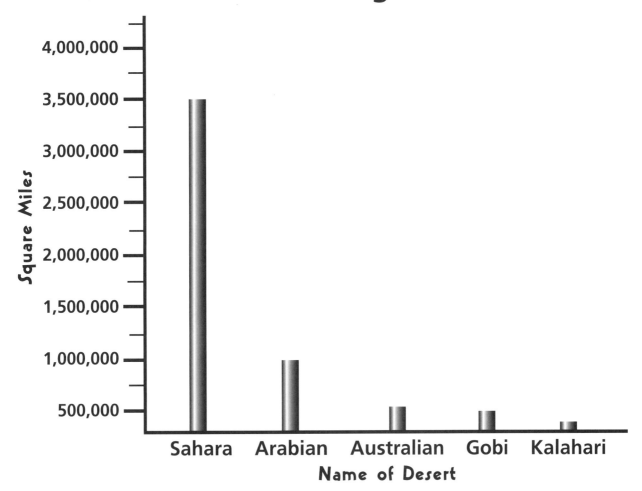

1 What is the subject of this graph? _____

2 How much bigger is the Sahara than
   the second largest desert on the graph? _____

3 Which is the third largest desert? _____

Teaching Tips...

Background

• Mathematical quantities and concepts can be represented symbolically and numerically in graphs. By constructing graphs learners will build a fundamental understanding of mathematical concepts and relationships such as amount and distance. Through graphing, learners will begin to create models for thinking about and solving problems. This will enhance learners' communication skills, allowing them to express their thinking to others.

Homework Helper

• Have a learner create a bar graph based on the heights of his or her family or friends. Have the learner color each bar in the graph a different color. When the graph is complete ask the student the following questions: Who is the tallest? Who is the shortest? What is the average height?

Research-based Activity

• Ask a learner to research on the Internet populations of cities within your state. Ask the learner to list the five most populous cities. Have the learner round the populations to the nearest 1,000, 5,000, or 10,000. Then ask the learner to create a pictograph using the population data. The learner can use a person symbol to represent a certain number of people.

Test Prep

• The following activities are based on a sampling of national and state standards. These standards challenge learners to be able to use raw data to construct various types of graphs such as bar graphs, pie charts, and pictographs. Learners should also be able to place data into and retrieve data from different types of graphs. Learners should also be comfortable changing and altering their graphs in order to project and predict results based upon ever-changing data.

Different Audiences

• If you are working with a challenged learner, you may want to focus on information that is personally interesting to the learner. Have the learner compose graphs based upon their favorite colors, books, animals, or games. Keep the amount of information to be graphed to a minimum. Add more information only after comprehension becomes easier.

Name _____

Favorite Fruit

A pictograph, or picture graph, shows information with pictures.

> **Directions:** Juniper is going to the store to buy her family fruit for the week. She needs to buy three oranges, three bunches of grapes, two apples, and four bananas. Help her to remember everything by placing an **X** in the pictograph for each piece of fruit she needs to buy.

X=1 piece of fruit

🍊	
🍇	X X X
🍎	
🍌	

FUN FACT

People have been enjoying apples for quite some time: Scientists estimate at least 750,000 years!

Name _____

A Trip to the Post Office

A bar graph uses bars to show information such as size or amount.

Directions: Every day thousands of letters are dropped off at post offices around America. These letters must be mailed to cities all over the country. Fill in the bar graph below to show how many letters were mailed from the post office on each day of the week.

Monday = 50 letters   Tuesday = 70 letters   Wednesday = 110 letters
Thursday = 40 letters   Friday = 90 letters

Days of the Week

FUN FACT

In 1775, Benjamin Franklin was named the first Postmaster General of the United States.

18

Name _____

Riding the Rails

A pie graph is a drawing of a circle divided into sections like pieces of a pie.

> **Directions:** The completion of the Transcontinental Railroad in 1869 made it possible for people to ship goods across America faster than ever before. Fill in the pie graph below using a different color to represent each product shipped. Use a different color for each product.

Plows = 4   Stoves = 4   Saddles = 10   Frying pans = 2

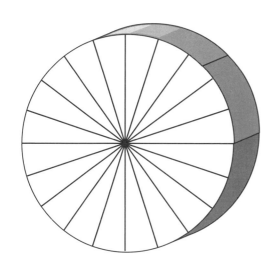

![FUN FACT]

When the Transcontinental Railroad was completed in 1869, the president of the Central Pacific Railroad, Leland Stanford, drove a golden spike into the last tie to mark the event.

Name _____

One-Horse Town

A pictograph, or picture graph, shows information with pictures.

> **Directions:** The mayor keeps forgetting how many businesses have set up shop in his colonial town. Help him remember by drawing the items in the following pictograph. Put your pictures anywhere in the town. In addition to the businesses shown below, add in 4 blacksmith shops, 3 dressmakers, 2 printers, and 2 shipbuilders.

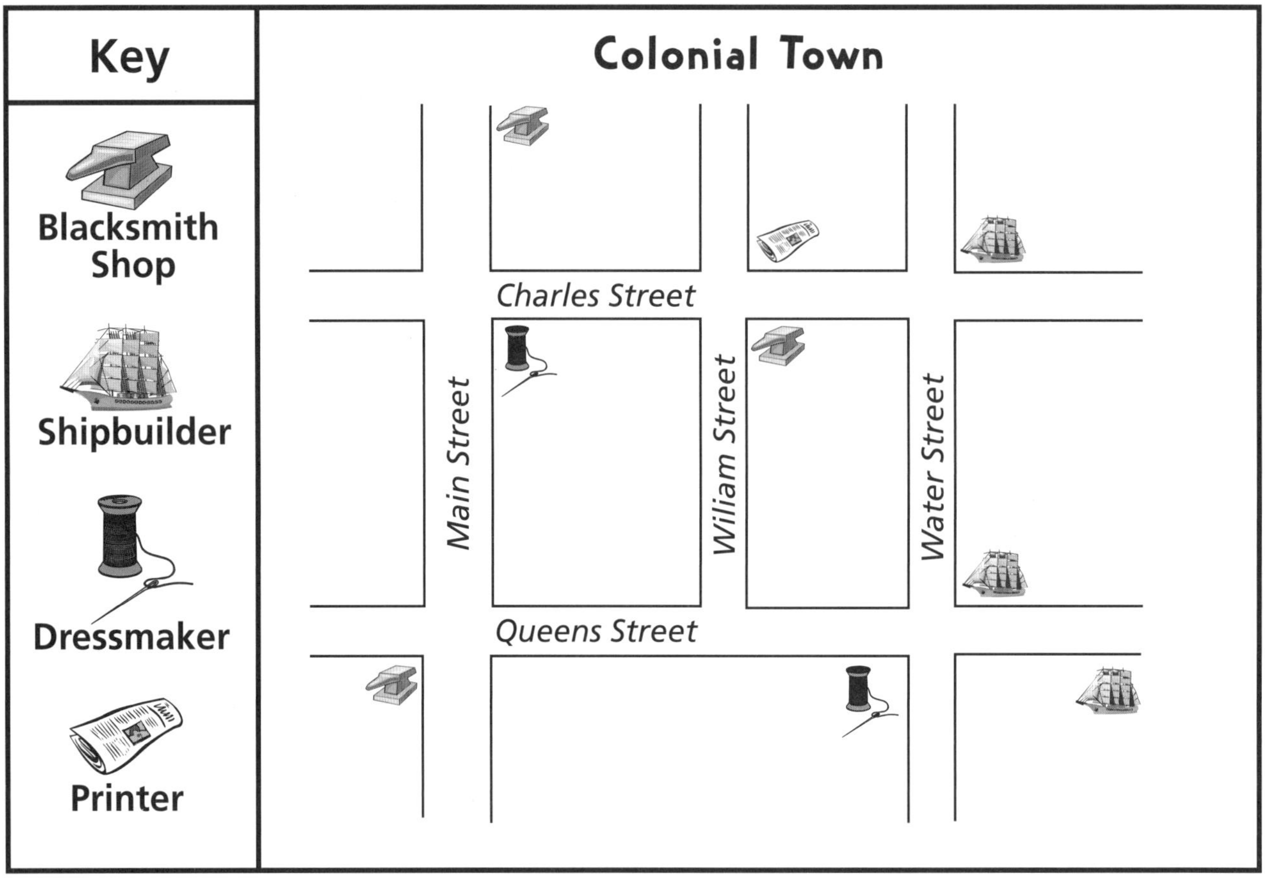

Key	Colonial Town
Blacksmith Shop	Charles Street
Shipbuilder	Main Street · Wiliam Street · Water Street
Dressmaker	Queens Street
Printer	

FUN FACT Children started working at a very young age in colonial America. Many boys began to learn blacksmithing at the age of 10.

Name _____

Skill Check—Graphing Data

Pie Graph

✏️⟹ **Directions:** Fill in the pie graph below. Use a different color for each after-school activity.

Number of Third Graders Participating in After-school Activities at Columbian Grammar School

Soccer = 4 students

Ice-skating = 2 students

Ballet = 2 students

Baseball = 8 students

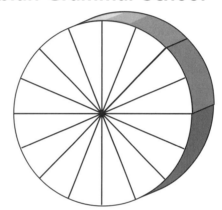

Bar Graph

✏️⟹ **Directions:** Becky took a poll of the students in her class to find out which flavor of ice cream is the most popular. Use Becky's results to fill in the bar graph below.

Vanilla = 7 students

Chocolate = 12 students

Rocky road = 3 students

Mint chip = 4 students

Strawberry = 2 students

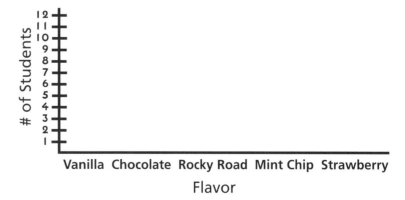

Teaching Tips...

TEACHING TIPS

Background

• Charts provide organized information, structured in a clear and logical manner. Giving learners the skills to read and interpret data within a chart allows them to equate mathematical concepts with the information provided. The ability to read charts allows learners to make connections and draw conclusions about various items of data.

Homework Helper

• Provide a learner with a chart that lists school supplies using symbols such as pens, pencils, erasers, rulers, notebooks. Have the learner count and list the supplies represented by the symbols in the chart. Ask the learner to use the information in the chart to solve mathematical problems such as: How many pens and pencils are there all together? What is the total number of supplies represented in the chart?

Research-based Activity

• Work with the learner, using the Internet to create a chart that shows the five-day predicted high and low temperatures for any city in the United States. Which city has the highest temperature for the week? Which city has the lowest temperature? What is the average high temperature of the learner's home town for the week?

Test Prep

• The following activities are based on a sampling of national and state standards. Such standards require learners to understand data represented in charts, compare and contrast the data, and be able to make predictions by following patterns which appear in the data.

Different Audiences

• For challenged learners, you may want to focus more upon the organization and representation of information within a chart rather than applying mathematical applications using the data. To challenge an accelerated learner, add more data categories to charts and have them use this information to focus on mathematical concepts, such as averaging.

Name _____

The Long, Hot Summer

A chart is used to organize data.

> **Directions:** The summer of 2003 was Lincoln City's hottest summer in 80 years. Study the weather chart below and answer the following questions.

Month	Average Daily Temperature	Average High Temperature	Average Low Temperature
June	84°	96°	72°
July	88°	102°	74°
August	90°	105°	75°
September	85°	99°	71°

1 What was the hottest month of the summer for Lincoln City? _____

2 During Lincoln City's hottest month, what was the average high temperature? _____

3 What month had the lowest average daily temperature? _____

4 What was the average daily temperature in June? _____

FUN FACT Whew, it's hot! The highest temperature ever recorded occurred in Death Valley, California. On July 10, 1913, a temperature of 134 degrees Fahrenheit was recorded there!

Name _____

Rainy Days

> **Directions:** Study the chart below and answer the following questions.

Amount of Rainfall

	Jan.	Feb.	March	April	May	June	July	Aug.	Sept.	Oct.	Nov.	Dec.
Valley View	0 inches	0.5 inches	1 inch	1 inch	.5 inches	0 inches	0 inches	1 inch	2 inches	0 inches	0.5 inches	0 inches
George Town	4 inches	4 inches	5 inches	6 inches	7 inches	4 inches	3 inches	2 inches	2 inches	0 inches	3 inches	3 inches

1 Does Valley View or George Town receive more rain each year? _____

2 What was the rainiest month of the year in Valley View? _____

3 What was the rainiest month of the year in George Town? _____

4 What was the total yearly amount of rainfall for Valley View? _____

FUN FACT

Don't forget your umbrella! Mount Waialeale, in Hawaii, is the rainiest and wettest spot on the planet. Mount Waialeale receives an average of 472 inches of rain each year. That's over 39 feet of rain!

Name _____

Here Comes the Sun

✏️▶ **Directions:** Use the chart to find the correct answers.

Month	Number of Sunny Days	Month	Number of Sunny Days
January	17	July	24
February	19	August	26
March	18	September	23
April	12	October	19
May	14	November	18
June	22	December	17

1 Which month had the most sunny days? _____

2 How many sunny days were
there in June and July together? _____

3 How many months had more than 20 sunny days? _____

4 How many months had fewer than 20 sunny days? _____

Extra Credit: Go on the Internet and find
the least sunny place on earth. Where is it? _____

FUN FACT

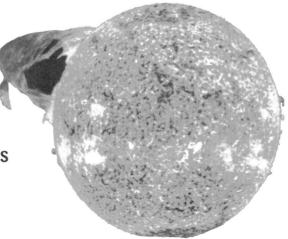

The world's
sunniest place is in the eastern
Sahara Desert, in Africa. It receives
an average of 11 hours and 46
minutes of sun each day.

Name _____

Aunt Judy's Garden

Directions: Aunt Judy plants a vegetable garden every summer, spring, and autumn. Use the chart below to answer the following questions.

	Summer	Spring	Autumn
Heads of lettuce	10	6	4
Ears of corn	2	4	12
Pumpkins	1	2	9
Bean plants	12	14	8

1 Did Aunt Judy grow more corn or beans? _____

2 Did Aunt Judy grow more beans
in the spring or in the autumn? _____

3 In which season did the
most vegetables grow? _____

4 Judy grew less than 5
pumpkins in which seasons? _____

The largest pumpkin ever grown was recorded at 1,131 pounds (513 kilograms)!

26

Name _____

Skill Check—Reading Charts

✏️➡ **Directions: Answer the following questions using the chart below.**

Eric, Bill, Lisa, and Joanne have decided to use all of the change they have been saving to buy movie tickets. Movie tickets are $10 each.

	# of pennies	# of nickels	# of dimes	# of quarters
Eric	45	40	15	8
Bill	70	55	40	12
Lisa	35	25	25	4
Joanne	10	35	60	24

1 Can Bill afford to buy a movie ticket? _____

2 How much more money would
Lisa need to buy a ticket? _____

✏️➡ **Directions: Answer the following questions using the chart below.**

Annie, Frank, and Julie went bird-watching and saw the following birds.

	Blackbirds	Bluejays	Robins	Cardinals
Annie	9	6	11	3
Frank	5	1	5	4
Julie	6	5	8	7

1 Who saw the most birds? _____

2 Who saw more bluejays, Frank
or Julie? How many more? _____

Teaching Tips...

Background

• Charts use symbols and numerals in a concisely organized manner to present data. Giving the learner the necessary tools to chart data allows him or her to grasp the ideas of practical representation and visual organization of data. A learner can then compare, contrast, and apply mathematical concepts to the data represented in charts. By organizing and charting information, learners begin to analyze and judge more involved elements of data. Skills such as these allow the learner to evaluate and communicate information and ideas.

Homework Helper

• Provide learners with a chart listing the amounts of time that it takes five different students to get to school. Round the times to the nearest minute. Have the learner time his or her trip to school, and add the data to the chart. You may want to ask the learner questions such as: Who has the longest trip? Who has the shortest trip? What is the average time of all the trips?

Research-based Activity

• To build on the activity on page 30, have the learner research on the Internet endangered sealife. He or she should compose a chart of five endangered animals. Data information could include number of animals remaining, and the increase or decrease in that number over the last year, five years, and ten years. Using the information in their chart, have the learner make predictions regarding the future prospects of each species' survival.

Test Prep

• National and state standards dictate that learners should be able to organize raw data into a chart. Learners should also be able to manipulate data within a chart based on mathematical concepts such as rounding and averaging.

Different Audiences

• For challenged learners, you may want to keep the number of chart categories small, at first. The categories can be increased as the learner gains confidence in his or her ability to understand the charting of data.

TEACHING TIPS

Name _____

Coming to America

A chart is a diagram used to show and compare information.

Directions: Fill in the chart below using the following information. Use the key to determine how many immigrants of different nationalities came to America. Fill in the chart, starting at the top, from highest to lowest numbers.

Ellis Island Immigration Records from 1790–1820

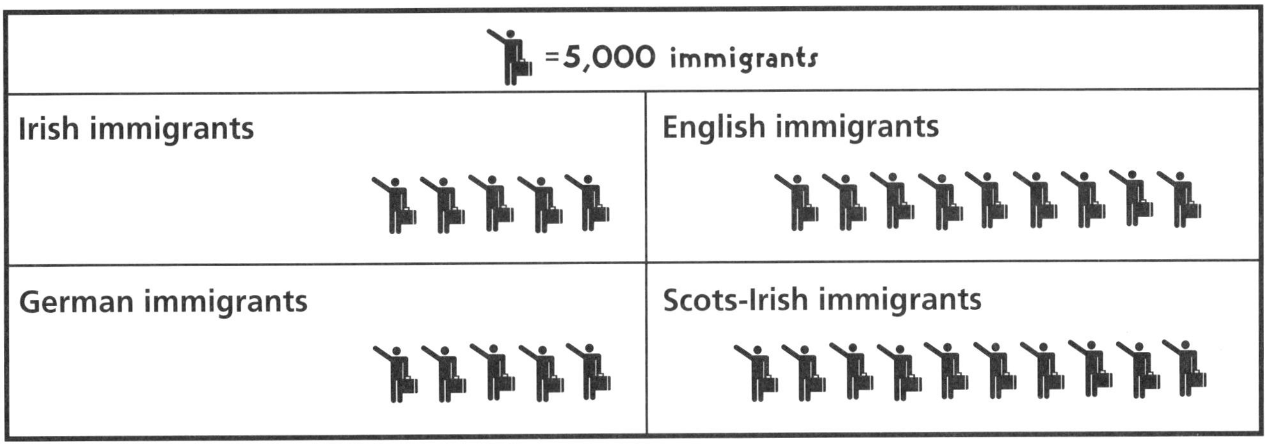

= 5,000 immigrants
Irish immigrants	English immigrants
German immigrants	Scots-Irish immigrants

Nationality	Number of Immigrants

Name _____

One Fish, Two Fish

A chart is a diagram used to show and compare information.

Directions: The oceans cover 71 percent of the surface of Earth. Earth's oceans are filled with fish, plants, and mammals. Look at the picture and fill in the chart below.

Type of Fish	Number in Picture	Fraction of Total Fish in Drawing
Little Fish		
Striped Fish		
Long Fish		
Jellyfish		

FUN FACT

The biggest fish in the ocean is the whale shark. Whale sharks can grow up to 50 feet long (15.24 meters) and weigh as much as 16 tons (16.26 metric tons)!

Name _____

Seeing the Forest

A chart is a diagram used to show and compare information.

> **Directions:** Mr. Toshio's class is taking a field trip to the state forest. Mr. Toshio has asked his students to count all the different kinds of trees they see and list them in order in the chart below. After you have placed the trees in order from highest to lowest, round the numbers of trees to the nearest 10.

Key 🌳 = Apple Tree 🌲 = Siberian Fir 🌴 = Italian Pine 🌲 = Evergreen 🌳 = White Acacia

Type of Tree	Number in Picture	Round to the Nearest 10

FUN FACT The world's tallest trees can be found in California. The giant redwood trees can reach over 100 meters in height. That's over 300 feet!

31

Name _____

Hot, Hot, Hot

✏️➡️ **Directions: August is the hottest month of the year in many parts of the United States. Study the weather map below and fill in the chart.**

Temperatures in Degrees on August 5th

80s   70s   60s   • Jonestown

• Imperial   • Crawford   73
85   74   • Stapleton

90s   69

• Sidney   • Indianola
83   • Allliance   84
77

100s

• Kimball   • Elk City   • Lincoln
100   92   86

• Rushville   • Danville
96   94

• North Fork
100s   101

Temperature in Degrees Fahrenheit	Number of Towns in Temperature Range	Town with Highest Temperature in Range
100°+		
90°–99°		
80°–89°		
70°–79°		
60°–69°		

FUN FACT

If you think it's hot where you live during the summer, try hanging out in the Sahara Desert. Summer temperatures there can rise to over 130 degrees Fahrenheit!

Name _____

Skill Check—Charting Data

Charting from Pictures

Directions: You are on a ship with scientists who are measuring the depth of different parts of the ocean. Study the drawing below and fill in the chart. After you have filled in the chart, round the last three digits of each number to the nearest hundred. The first couple have been done to get you started.

560   4,240   6,990   23,850   35,320   17,450   12,667   7,210   2,880   890

Ocean Depths in Feet

560	feet	600
890	feet	900
	feet	
	feet	
	feet	
	feet	
	feet	
	feet	
	feet	
	feet	

© Rosen School Supply•Brain Builders Mathematical Thinking: Ideas/Procedures•3•RSS

Teaching Tips...

TEACHING TIPS

Background

- Tables use columns and rows to organize mathematical information. The ability to interpret and understand tables is essential to recognizing mathematical concepts such as the multiplication of numbers through the organization of answers in a multiplication table. Understanding tables helps learners to more easily interpret large amounts of data and to see patterns and relationships among numbers. Many mathematical concepts become much more accessible to learners after they become more fluent in the language of tabling.

Homework Helper

- Ask a learner to copy the multiplication chart on page 36. Have the learner change the first column's numbers from 1 through 9 to 10 through 90. Work with the learner to see the patterns emerge: The answers all change in the same way as a zero is added to each of them.

Research-based Activity

- Ask the learner to go on the Internet and research an important historical mathematician, such as Pythagoras or Euclid.

Test Prep

- National and state standards have been used to create the following activities. Learners should be able to both read and understand tables and fill in missing information. The learner should be comfortable with retrieving specific information from a table.

Different Audiences

- For challenged learners, you may want to provide complete tables, and develop questions that focus on retrieving information. Using fewer number columns will help. The columns can be increased as the learner becomes more comfortable in retrieving data.

Name _____

Add It Up!

A table organizes mathematical information into columns and rows.

> **Directions: Complete the addition tables below by filling in the missing numbers.**

+	0	1	2	3	4	5	6	7	8	9	10
0											
1					5						
2			4								
3						8					
4							10				
5						10					
6										15	
7							13				
8										17	
9				13							
10				13							

+	0	5	10	50	100
0					
5			15		
10					
15		20			
20				70	
25					
30			40		
35		40			
40					140
45					
50			60		

Name _____

They're Multiplying

A table organizes mathematical information into columns and rows.

Directions: Use the multiplication table below to answer the following questions.

X	1	2	3	4	5	6	7	8	9
1	1	2	3	4	5	6	7	8	9
2	2	4	6	8	10	12	14	16	18
3	3	6	9	12	15	18	21	24	27
4	4	8	12	16	20	24	28	32	36
5	5	10	15	20	25	30	35	40	45
6	6	12	18	24	30	36	42	48	54
7	7	14	21	28	35	42	49	56	63
8	8	16	24	32	40	48	56	64	72
9	9	18	27	36	45	54	63	72	81

1 When you multiply an odd number by an
   even number, is the answer odd or even? _____

2 When you multiply an odd number by an
   odd number, is the answer odd or even? _____

3 What happens to a number
   when it is multiplied by one? _____

36

Name _____

Solve to Chart

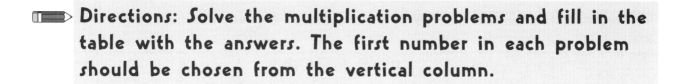

Directions: Solve the multiplication problems and fill in the table with the answers. The first number in each problem should be chosen from the vertical column.

1 x 4 = _____	7 x 3 = _____
2 x 3 = _____	8 x 3 = _____
2 x 5 = _____	9 x 3 = _____
3 x 6 = _____	9 x 4 = _____
4 x 6 = _____	9 x 5 = _____
5 x 5 = _____	9 x 6 = _____
6 x 4 = _____	

Draw a line through the numbers that you have filled in on the chart.

X	1	2	3	4	5	6	7	8	9
1									
2									
3									
4									
5									
6									
7									
8									
9									

Name _____

Something's Missing

✏️➤ **Directions: Fill in the missing numbers to complete the table.**

X	0	5	10	15	20
1			10	15	
2	0	10			40
3				45	
4	0		40	60	80
5	0	25		75	
6	0	30	60	90	120
7	0			105	140
8	0	40	80	120	
9	0	45		135	180

Name _____

Skill Check—Tables

Addition

✏️ **Fill in the addition table.**

+	75	122	277	488
50				
99	174		376	
125				
266				754
311		433		
499				
535			812	

Multiplication

✏️ **Complete the multiplication table by filling in the missing numbers.**

X	3	6	9
1			
2			
3			
4			36
5			
6			
7		42	
8			
9			81
10	30		

Solving Problems

✏️ **Fill in the multiplication table. Solve the multiplication problems and fill in the table with the answers.**

1 x 2 = _____

3 x 4 = _____

5 x 6 = _____

8 x 9 = _____

X	1	2	3	4	5	6	7	8	9
1									
2									
3									
4									
5									
6									
7									
8									
9									

Draw a line through the numbers that you have filled in on the chart.

Teaching Tips...

TEACHING TIPS

Background

• By tackling activities that involve visual puzzles, learners strengthen their ability to read, interpret, and mathematically manipulate data. Becoming skilled at interpreting visual data helps the learner to use concepts such as representation and visualization to solve mathematical problems.

Homework Helper

• Having learners play the game battleship might be a fun way to reinforce what they have learned about grids in such activities as Stew's Grades (pg. 44).

Research-based Activity

• Ask a learner to use the Internet to find the populations of five states. Have the learner round the numbers to the nearest 100,000. Help the learner to mark off increments of 100,000, and ask the learner to make a bar graph using the population figures. Ask the learner to interpret the graph by having her or him answer questions about the results.

Test Prep

• The following activities are based on a sampling of national and state standards. Learners should be comfortable reading and interpreting the data shown in charts and graphs in order to solve visual puzzles.

Different Audiences

• Challenge accelerated learners by having them design their own graphs, charts, or grids using subject matter that they find interesting. They can pull information from the Internet.

Name _____

Sharks!

✏️➤ **Directions:** Color in one box for each type of shark that Ms. Perez's class saw at the aquarium. We've started you off with Mako sharks.

Mako sharks = 3
Great white sharks = 2
Hammerhead sharks = 5
Tiger sharks = 4
Whale sharks = 3

Mako sharks					
Great white sharks					
Hammerhead sharks					
Tiger sharks					
Whale sharks					

1 How many sharks are there all together? _____

2 What is the total of tiger and whale sharks? _____

3 How many more hammerhead sharks are there than whale sharks? _____

FUN FACT

Sharks have one of the best senses of smell of any animal. Sharks can smell from great distances. In fact, two-thirds of a shark's brain is dedicated just to smelling!

41

Name _____

Out of the Wild!

A bar graph uses bars to show amounts or numbers so that they can be compared.

✏️ **Directions: Janey is taking a survey to find out her classmates' favorite wild animals. She marked down her results in the chart below. Use the numbers from the chart to fill in the bar graph.**

Wild Animal	Number of students who like the animal best
Tigers	3
Pandas	2
Horses	5
Sharks	3
Monkeys	4
Eagles	1

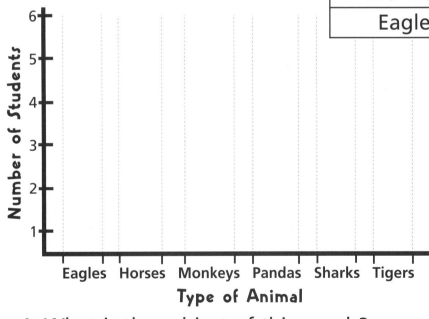

1 What is the subject of this graph? _____

2 What animal do most of Janey's classmates like? _____

3 How many classmates does Janey have? _____

Name _____

Gold!

A pie graph is a drawing of a circle divided into sections like pieces of a pie.

> **Directions: Study the information below and fill in the pie graph. Give each miner a slice of the pie that matches the amount of gold nuggets that they found. Color in each miner's slice with a different color.**

Gold Nuggets Found at Big Bear Creek in July 1850

Joe Wilson = 4 nuggets
Bill Evans = 2 nuggets
José Morales = 4 nuggets
Mary Clark = 5 nuggets
Charles Pepin = 3 nuggets
Jack Birch = 2 nuggets
Total nuggets found at Big Bear Creek = 20

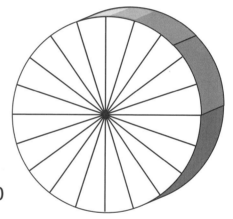

1. Which miner found the most nuggets? What fraction of all the nuggets did he or she find? _____

2. What fraction of all the nuggets were found by José Morales? _____

3. If the miners found three times as many nuggets at Big Bear Creek during August, how many nuggets would that be? _____

Name _____

Stew's Grades

A grid gives information from left to right, from top to bottom. By using this information, we can plot points in the area of a grid.

Directions: Stew wants to find out what his math grade is. Follow these instructions to help him.

Draw a dot on (1,B).
Draw a dot on (3,C).
Draw a dot on (6,D).
Draw a dot on (3,E).
Draw a dot on (1,F).

1 Connect the dots in the order you made them. What is Stew's grade?

2 Explain how you found (1,F) on the grid.

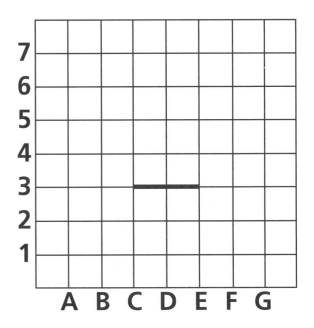

FUN FACT

Did you know that eggs and butter get graded too? The U.S. government uses a grading system based on the quality of foods like eggs and butter.

Name _____

Skill Check—Visual Puzzles

Bar Graph

 Directions: Show the temperatures of each city on the bar graph.

San Diego 78°   Bismarck 54°
Austin 66°   Kansas City 62°

1 Which city has the highest temperature? _____

2 What is the difference in degrees between the highest and lowest temperatures?

_____

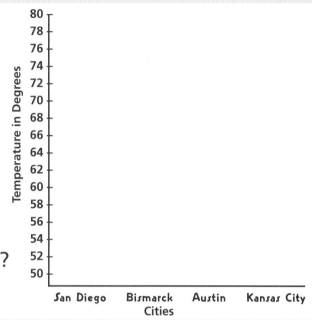

Grids

 Directions: Steve loves his rugby shirt because it has his favorite number on it. Follow the directions to find out what Steve's favorite number is.

Draw a dot on (3,B).
Draw a dot on (6,E).
Draw a dot on (1,E).

1 Connect the dots in the order you made them. What is Steve's favorite number? _____

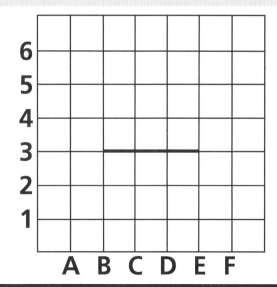

Answer Key

p. 4
1) airplane, 5 miles
2) 2 miles
3) 1 mile
4) 15 miles

p. 5
1) praying mantis
2) 3
3) 28 cm

p. 6
1) John, 90 lbs
2) 60 lbs, 140 lbs
3) 40 lbs

p. 7

	Monday	Tuesday	Wednesday	Friday
Sarah	$3.10	$2.50	$1.75	$5.40
Mindy	$2.50	$4.80	$2.70	$3.25

p. 8

+	0	1	2	3	4	5
0	0	1	2	3	4	5
1	1	2	3	4	5	6
2	2	3	4	5	6	7
3	3	4	5	6	7	8
4	4	5	6	7	8	9
5	5	6	7	8	9	10

X	1	2	3	4	5
1	1	2	3	4	5
2	2	4	6	8	10
3	3	6	9	12	15
4	4	8	12	16	20
5	5	10	15	20	25

1) even
2) The number stays the same.

p. 9
1) Vietnam Veterans Memorial, 400
2) The Tomb of the Unknown Soldier

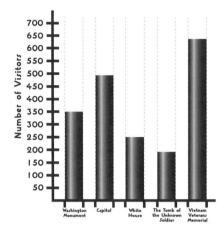

p. 11
1) 6
2) Pikes's Peak
3) Aconcagua

p. 12
1) 5 pets
2) 10
3) 3rd grade, 15
4) 60
5) 2nd grade, 5th grade

p. 13
1) boa constrictors
2) 1/2
3) 1/8
4) 1/4

p. 14
1) the number of moons of each planet
2) Saturn, 30
3) Venus

p. 15
1) the sizes of the world's largest deserts
2) 2,500,000 square miles
3) Australian

p. 17

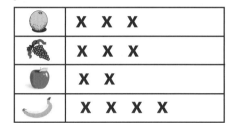

p. 18

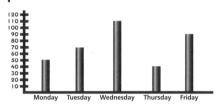

p. 19

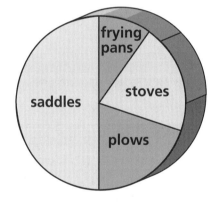

(Placement of sections may vary.)

p. 20
Placement of items will vary.

46

p. 21 Pie graph

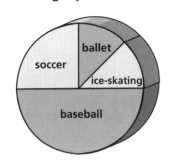

(Placement of sections will vary.)

Bar graph

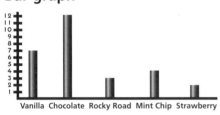

p. 23
1) August
2) 105°
3) June
4) 84°

p. 24
1) George Town
2) September
3) May
4) 6.5 inches

p. 25
1) August
2) 46
3) 4
4) 8
Extra Credit: the South Pole

p. 26
1) beans
2) spring
3) autumn
4) summer and spring

p. 27 Movie Tickets
1) yes

2) $4.90

Bird-watching
1) Annie
2) Julie, 4

p. 29

Nationality	Number of Immigrants
Scots-Irish	50,000
English	45,000
Irish	25,000
German	25,000

p. 30

Type of fish	Number in Picture	Fraction of Total Fish in Drawing
Little Fish	10	1/4
Striped Fish	5	1/8
Long Fish	5	1/8
Jellyfish	20	1/2

p. 31

Type of tree	Number in Picture	Round to the Nearest 10
Siberian Fir	17	20
White Acacia	15	20
Evergreen	12	10
Apple Tree	8	10
Italian Pine	5	10

p. 32

Temperature in Degrees Fahrenheit	Number of Towns in Temperature Range	Town with Highest Temperature in Range
100+	2	North Fork
90-99	3	Rushville
80-89	4	Lincoln
70-79	3	Alliance
60-69	1	Stapleton

p. 33

Ocean Depth from Shallowest to Deepest	Last Three Digits Rounded
560	600
890	900
2,880	2,900
4,240	4,200
6,990	7,000
7,210	7,200
12,667	12,700
17,450	17,500
23,850	23,900
35,320	35,300

p. 35

+	0	1	2	3	4	5	6	7	8	9	10
0	0	1	2	3	4	5	6	7	8	9	10
1	1	2	3	4	5	6	7	8	9	10	11
2	2	3	4	5	6	7	8	9	10	11	12
3	3	4	5	6	7	8	9	10	11	12	13
4	4	5	6	7	8	9	10	11	12	13	14
5	5	6	7	8	9	10	11	12	13	14	15
6	6	7	8	9	10	11	12	13	14	15	16
7	7	8	9	10	11	12	13	14	15	16	17
8	8	9	10	11	12	13	14	15	16	17	18
9	9	10	11	12	13	14	15	16	17	18	19
10	10	11	12	13	14	15	16	17	18	19	20

+	0	5	10	50	100
0	0	5	10	50	100
5	5	10	15	55	105
10	10	15	20	60	110
15	15	20	25	65	115
20	20	25	30	70	120
25	25	30	35	75	125
30	30	35	40	80	130
35	35	40	45	85	135
40	40	45	50	90	140
45	45	50	55	95	145
50	50	55	60	100	150

p. 36
1) even
2) odd
3) It stays the same.

p. 37

X	1	2	3	4	5	6	7	8	9
1				4					
2			6		10				
3						18			
4						24			
5					25				
6				24					
7			21						
8			24						
9			27	36	45	54			

p. 38

X	0	5	10	15	20
1	0	5	10	15	20
2	0	10	20	30	40
3	0	15	30	45	60
4	0	20	40	60	80
5	0	25	50	75	100
6	0	30	60	90	120
7	0	35	70	105	140
8	0	40	80	120	160
9	0	45	90	135	180

p. 39 Addition

+	75	122	277	488
50	125	172	327	538
99	174	221	376	587
125	200	247	402	613
266	341	388	543	754
311	386	433	588	799
499	574	621	776	987
535	610	657	812	1023

Multiplication

X	3	6	9
1	3	6	9
2	6	12	18
3	9	18	27
4	12	24	36
5	15	30	45
6	18	36	54
7	21	42	63
8	24	48	72
9	27	54	81
10	30	60	90

Solving Problems

X	1	2	3	4	5	6	7	8	9
1	1	2	3	4	5	6	7	8	9
2	2	4	6	8	10	12	14	16	18
3	3	6	9	12	15	18	21	24	27
4	4	8	12	16	20	24	28	32	36
5	5	10	15	20	25	30	35	40	45
6	6	12	18	24	30	36	42	48	54
7	7	14	21	28	35	42	49	56	63
8	8	16	24	32	40	48	56	64	72
9	9	18	27	36	45	54	63	72	81

p. 41

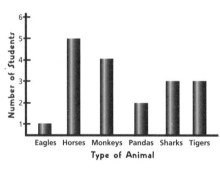

Mako sharks				
Great white sharks				
Hammerhead sharks				
Tiger sharks				
Whale sharks				

1) 17
2) 7
3) 2

p. 42

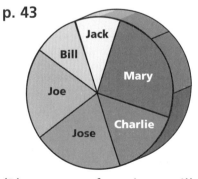

1) Favorite animals of Janey's classmates
2) horses
3) 18

p. 43

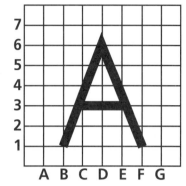

(Placement of sections will vary.)

1) Mary Clark, 1/4
2) 1/5
3) 60

p. 44

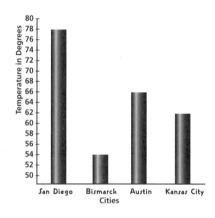

1) A
2) Answers will vary.

p. 45 Bar Graph

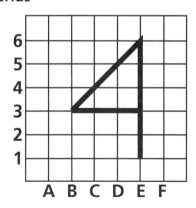

1) San Diego
2) 24 degrees

Grids

1) 4